THE MASAI

Also by the same author

THE APACHE INDIANS
Raiders of the Southwest

THE AZTEC
Indians of Mexico

THE CHEROKEE
Indians of the Mountains

THE CHIPPEWA INDIANS
Rice Gatherers of the Great Lakes

THE CROW INDIANS
Hunters of the Northern Plains

THE DELAWARE INDIANS
Eastern Fishermen and Farmers

THE ESKIMO
Arctic Hunters and Trappers

HORSEMEN OF THE WESTERN PLATEAUS
The Nez Percé Indians

THE INCA
Indians of the Andes

INDIANS OF THE LONGHOUSE
The Story of the Iroquois

THE MAYA
Indians of Central America

THE MISSION INDIANS OF CALIFORNIA

THE NAVAJO
Herders, Weavers, and Silversmiths

THE PUEBLO INDIANS
Farmers of the Rio Grande

THE SEA HUNTERS
Indians of the Northwest Coast

THE SEMINOLE INDIANS

THE SIOUX INDIANS
Hunters and Warriors of the Plains

THE MASAI

Herders of
East Africa

SONIA BLEEKER

Illustrated by
KISA N. SASAKI

William Morrow & Co.
New York • 1963

Grateful recognition is given to Alan H. Jacobs of the University of Illinois, for reading and criticizing the manuscript.

CONTENTS

ONE

THE MASAI OF EAST AFRICA

The tall, handsome Masai (mah-sigh') of East Africa are cattlemen. They are slender, long-limbed, brown-skinned people with well-shaped heads, fine features, and black, kinky hair. About 75 years ago the Masai may have numbered between 12,500 and 25,000 people. They now number close to 115,000. The vast, high plains of Masailand, which stretch across the equator in eastern Africa, are dry grasslands. They are the grazing grounds for the largest and most varied number of wild animals in the world. These grasslands are also good for cattle, which can graze along with the wild animals.

The Masai, who call themselves Il-Maasai, own large herds of cattle, sheep, and goats, which give them all they need to live on, and they are proud of them. Their warriors say, "God in the olden days gave us all the cattle upon the earth. It is, therefore, unworthy of a Masai man or woman to dig the earth to grow crops."

The Masai firmly believe that their African neighbors, whether farmers or cattlemen like themselves, got their cattle from them. They think these neighbors either stole Masai cattle or kept the strays that escaped from their herds. For this reason Masai warriors trained for many centuries, so they could prevent raiders from stealing their cattle and could raid their neighbors' herds to recover so-called stolen cattle. The neighbors who fought and often killed these fearless men dreaded the raids. In the past, several African peoples were so badly defeated by the Masai that they had to give up their lands. They gradually gave up herding, too, and turned to farming. Thus the Masai became an important power in East Africa and acquired much territory. However, several peoples, among them the Kikuyu, the Kamba, and the Nandi, to the north of Masailand, bravely met the Masai warriors time after time, fought them, and chased them off their lands. Both sides kept fighting despite losses in men and cattle.

A Masai warrior wanted no more glorious end than to be speared and clubbed by an enemy in battle or in a raid, so long as the raid was successful. If unsuccessful, the men were ashamed to return to the warrior villages, their *manyattas*. "To be defeated and to die is the same," they said.

The reputation of the Masai as fierce fighters was further spread by their neighbors, so that when the white explorers first came to East Africa in the 1880's, they were warned that the lands of

the Masai were the most dangerous. Many explorers avoided them. In this way, the neighbors,
as well as the Masai, were left alone.

The Masai have no written history. Their past
has been pieced together from their many stories
of how their people came to be and of their wanderings, and from their myths and legends. Their
language has been studied, and through it we have
found other people related to the Masai, because
they speak a similar language. The people most
closely related to them are the Karamojong and
the Nandi. It was believed at one time that all
these people came into the Rift Valley from
around the Nile River. So they were called
Nilotes. Now, however, new archeological evi-
dence suggests that the ancestors of the Masai may
have migrated from southern Ethiopia. It is,
therefore, more correct to call the Masai and their
neighbors Nilo-Hamitic. The Hamitic people are
a large African group that includes the Tuareg

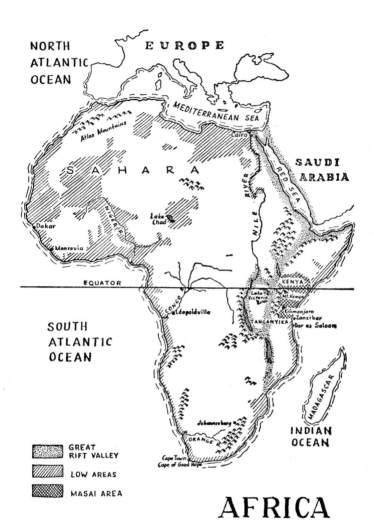

NORTH
ATLANTIC
OCEAN

EUROPE

MEDITERRANEAN SEA

Atlas Mountains

Cairo

SAUDI
ARABIA

S A H A R A

NILE RIVER

RED SEA

NIGER R.

Dakar

Lake
Chad

Monrovia

EQUATOR

KENYA

Lake
Victoria

Mt. Kenya

CONGO

Léopoldville

Kilimanjaro

Zanzibar

SOUTH
ATLANTIC
OCEAN

TANGANYIKA

Dar es Salaam

MADAGASCAR

INDIAN
OCEAN

Johannesburg

ORANGE R.

Cape Town
Cape of Good Hope

GREAT
RIFT VALLEY

LOW AREAS

MASAI AREA

AFRICA

and Berbers of the Sahara, the Egyptians, and many Ethiopian tribes.

The Rift Valley is like a land funnel, or trough. At one end it lies between the East Horn on the Gulf of Aden and the Red Sea. The sides of this giant trough rise 2000 feet and over, above a floor that is itself 2000 feet above sea level in many places. The Rift Valley leads to the lake region in the interior of southeast Africa. In some areas it is quite wide—as much as 50 miles. The Ethiopian highlands rise to the east on one side; the East African highlands, to the southwest. The world-famous mountains, Mount Kilimanjaro, over 19,000 feet, and Mount Kenya, over 17,000 feet, are located here.

Here, too, are the awesome volcanic formations, or volcanic massif, as the Africans call it, of the Crater Highlands. They rise over 11,000 feet above the great Rift Valley. In the same region is the Olduvai Gorge, where the archeologists, Dr. and Mrs. Leakey, found the famous Zinjanthropus skull. The skull may be two million years old—the oldest human remains ever found.

This picturesque land rises from dry, treeless, grassy plains and thorn-bush areas to rain forests and bamboo, and to mountain moorland. All the flora and fauna are different and interesting to visitors. On the high ground live the mountain reedbuck and the giant forest hog; in the plains below, the wildebeest, zebra, topi, antelope, lion, and cheetah. The buffalo, rhinoceros, and leopard still roam everywhere, as they have for thousands of years.

Scientists today think the Masai have lived in Masailand for well over a thousand years. According to Masai legends, however, their wanderings date back only about three hundred years. They were then already full-fledged herdsmen, with domesticated cattle and milch cows. They were able to live off their cattle entirely. Their additional needs, such as vegetables and grains and a few skins for clothing, were minor. Able to rely on their herds for all their needs, the Nilo-

Hamites remained nomads, moving freely about in search of pasture. They began to penetrate southward below the equator. The Bantu people around the shores of Lake Victoria stopped their advance. So the cattlemen went to the southeast, pushing out the weaker Bushmanoid hunters. They encircled and scattered farming communities of Cushites, who are also Hamitic, and drove them toward the mountainous sections. The Masai warriors married Cushites, so that today their language has many Cushitic additions.

The Masai have kept in their midst a few groups of the hunters they conquered, and permit them to live on the land. These hunters are now called the Dorobo. They manage to live with the Masai and support themselves by hunting and by trading skins and ivory with the Masai for milk, blood, and meat.

One group of Masai, which lost its cattle to another raiding Masai group, turned to the land and became excellent farmers. Today we know these Masai farmers as Arusha, or Iloikop. They still speak the same language as the pastoral, or herding, Masai and trade farm products with them. As a rule the Masai herdsmen part only with their scrawniest and oldest heads, so they can safely say that the Arusha cattle are of poor stock. The Arusha, they say proudly, do not know how to raise cattle.

The Arusha farmers grow a great variety of grains and, in addition to cattle, they raise sheep and goats. They grow sorghum and millet, which is a kind of cereal. The Arusha make beer out of millet, and this, too, is good for trading, since the Masai like beer. They also grow Eleusine, or raggee, cotton, hemp, and ambary. The flour made made from Eleusine seeds is somewhat bitter, but it is an important food. Coarse cloth and rope are made from both hemp and ambary fibers. The Arusha grow the cowpea, a close relative of the bean; okra for stews; hyacinth beans, a climbing vine with purple flowers and edible beanlike seeds; and sesame (ses'ah-mee). From the pounded sesame seeds they make an oil, important in cooking. From India they have imported and learned to grow Jew's mallow and pigeon peas; from Malaya, bananas and sweet yams; from the Americas, gourds, corn, manioc, peanuts, sweet potatoes, and tobacco.

The Masai lands are a belt of dry, dusty, golden, sun-baked grass. During the wet season the grass turns into a thick green carpet, on which their cattle fatten. But during the dry season, the Masai move their herds toward the highlands and mountains in search of pasture. They do this also to give the grass in the lowlands a chance to survive until the rainy season returns. Grass is of great value to the Masai because of their cattle. They revere both as gifts from God, saying, "God gave us cattle and grass. Cattle are in our hearts. Their smell is sweet to us." When one Masai greets another, he will say, "I hope your cattle are well."

The Masai language is rich in words concerning cattle. They have many words for the colors and shades of hides. They have words that exactly describe the shape and length of horns and words for

measuring the height and sleekness of the cattle.
Therefore, a man can describe his cattle, sheep,
and goats with the minutest detail, and he can
recognize them in the midst of any herd. Should
a bullock go astray, the herder knows its color,
spots, size, age, and branding marks. If the animal
has not been killed or eaten, it will be found.

The cattle that the Masai herd originated in
India and northeastern Africa and gradually
worked their way through the Rift Valley to
southern Kenya and Tanganyika. In this tropical
zone they did not thrive because of the tsetse fly,
but still they managed to survive. These cattle are
a cross between the Mediterranean cattle, which
first appeared in Egypt some ten thousand years
B.C., and the humped zebu cattle of India, which
reached Egypt less than four thousand years ago.
They did not spread southward to East Africa for
about three thousand years.

The Masai, therefore, have probably been
herders, as a sole occupation, for about a thousand
years. Woolly sheep were introduced even later

than cattle, and were a result of European coloni-
zation. African sheep grow hair instead of wool
and have fat tails. The most widespread animal in
Africa, as in the rest of the world, is the dog. Goats
are second in number.

The Masai cattle, sheep, and goats are domesticated, so that the Masai can raise all the meat they
want, provided they have enough pasture land.
Each herd owner is careful to keep a few select
bulls for breeding. Milch cows and their calves
also receive excellent care. Of these a few male
calves will in time become breeding bulls, too. The
other male calves are castrated and, as beef steers
or bullocks, are bled periodically when the Masai
want to drink blood. The steers are also used for
meat. The Masai butcher them with the greatest
reluctance. Cattle are not only food, they are
wealth. A man who owns large herds commands
great respect and can support many wives and
children.

The food of the Masai is mainly milk, meat,
and blood. Milk mixed with a tiny amount of

cow's urine curdles into a soft cheese. But because Masai cows are not as well fed as ours, they do not yield as much milk. A woman makes sure that the calves have had enough before she milks the cow or cows to feed her family. The daily yield per cow is about a quart of milk. In the dry season there may be no more than a half a pint after the calf is fed, and sometimes none is left. Then the Masai drink blood to supplement the diet. During the wet season when milk is plentiful, they still like to drink some blood. They say it helps digestion.

The Masai do not kill an animal to get its blood, which they like to drink while it is still fresh and warm. Instead they tie a leather thong around the neck of a bullock, so the jugular vein will bulge out. While one or two men hold the animal, a third shoots an arrow into its neck. The arrow strikes the animal's jugular vein, but the man makes sure it does not penetrate too deeply. As the arrow is pulled out, the blood flows into a gourd, held under the wound. They take no more than a quart of blood from a bullock at one time. The skin over the wound is then pressed together with dung to stop the bleeding. At most, an animal is bled once a month. Its owner prefers to bleed the animal only when it has been thriving on good grass during the wet season, which lasts about four or five months a year.

Should a bullock or cow die, its blood is drawn immediately and drunk. Immediately, too, the warm contents of the stomach are eaten. The people cut up the meat and roast it. Otherwise, a cattle owner goes without meat for a week or two at a time and often longer, before he overcomes his reluctance to reduce his wealth by butchering one of his herd.

Although the Masai drink milk mixed with blood, they do not drink milk and eat meat together, nor do they put meat into a gourd that has held milk. Before they eat meat, the Masai make sure that a period of time has elapsed since they last drank milk. A person who does eat meat and drink milk on the same day is considered a glutton. The Masai believe that a glutton's cows will stop giving milk.

Honey is one of the favorite foods of the Masai. Their youngsters, like youngsters the world over, like sweets and are very fond of wild honey right out of the comb. The elders drink honey wine, which is fermented honey. A man or woman who wishes to make some wine takes the honey to a separate hut and spends from a week to ten days brewing it. Honey wine is served at all ceremonies, but neither warriors nor young people drink it even then.

Today the farming Masai, the Arusha, raise some honeybees. But in the past both the Arusha and the pastoral Masai depended entirely on the birds of their grasslands to guide them to beehives. These birds have been called honey guides, or indicators. Like the Masai, the honey guides are nomads. They lay their eggs in other birds' nests and let other birds raise their young for them. So the adult honey guides are not tied down by nests and young and are free to wander over the grass-lands south of the Sahara. These small, dull-colored, gray-to-brownish African birds are the size of our sparrow and have short bills. Their flight is strong and swift.

The honey guide feeds on insects, mostly on bees and wasps. To get honey, it flies near a person, or an animal that also likes honey, and chatters loudly to attract attention. Once the honey guide sees it is being followed, it flies to a beehive. The bird

starts picking at the hive. Then it perches on a nearby branch and waits until the person or animal has dug up the bees' nest, scattered the bees, and taken the honey or, in the case of an animal, eaten it. The little bird then moves in to feast on the honeycomb itself. It has been found that the honey guide's stomach bacteria can digest the wax of the honeycomb.

The Masai, grateful to the honey guide, always leave a goodly portion of the honeycomb for the bird. They believe that should they fail to leave enough, the bird will never guide them to honey again. Instead it may lead them, with friendly chatter, straight to a lion's den or to a poisonous snake.

Even people temporarily confined to their camps by the fear of the tsetse fly will risk being bitten by the fly just to get honey. A head medicine man's diet is usually restricted to milk and honey —with some goat liver as an occasional treat—so the honey is important. As people get older, sweets become a necessary part of their limited diet.

On the whole the Masai eat much less than we do. Their average caloric intake per person is about 1300 calories a day, while ours is closer to 3000. In the past active warriors averaged about 2000 calories a day while preparing for a raid.

A first glimpse of the Masai was reported by a British explorer, Joseph Thomson, who courageously undertook to explore their lands in 1882, when he was twenty-six years old. Traveling westward from the port of Mombasa in southern Kenya, Thomson made his journey to the Masai territory on foot. He had been warned, of course, of the dangers ahead, and carried extra packs, bundles, and boxes of iron and copper wire, knives, beads, and cloth as gifts for the Masai warriors. He hoped to get their permission to pass peacefully through their lands. The expedition moved warily, although Thomson and a few of his companions were heavily armed. They knew the Masai had spears and clubs, but no guns.

In 1882 wild animals grazed over the African

plains as far as the eye could see. To Europeans, whose zoos then were not as large as they are today, these animals were an unforgettable spectacle.

"Great herds of buffalo were moving from these grazing grounds toward the shelter and coolness of the forest in the distance for their daily snooze and rumination," Thomson reported. He counted three such large herds. Since the Masai were not hunters and did not especially like the meat of wildlife, the animals had no fear of men and permitted the explorers to approach at close range.

As the buffalo herds passed, enormous numbers of wildebeest (will'd-beest), which we call gnu, continued their peaceful grazing or galloped about clumsily, waving their tails. The wildebeest are horned animals that look fierce, like our Texas longhorns, but are actually harmless. Mingling with them were sturdy zebras—plump, striped, horselike creatures. There were tawny, spotted giraffes, graceful in the distance, nibbling at shrubbery, which was probably acacia, and kick-

ing up the dust playfully as they followed one
another. Farther on in the lowlands Thomson saw
rhinoceros, their single long horn making them
look dangerous, ready to fight. On a ridge farther
away were a watchful troop of ostriches, prepared
to scud away at the slightest alarm. The ostrich
had good reason to fear man, since the Masai
prized their feathers for ornaments and head-
dresses. There was also a herd of hartebeests—
grayish brown antelopes. With them were graceful brown-and-white impalas—another African

antelope. The impalas seemed to float in the air as they leaped about.

At a line of trees that marked the flow of a stream were waterbuck—still another kind of African antelope—leisurely feeding in two's and three's in the rich grass. They frightened away a water hog, which scooted off with tail erect.

Near the borders of Masailand rumors began to spread that 2000 Masai warriors were en route to meet the expedition. The African carriers were so frightened of meeting the Masai that many of them lay down on the trail, unable to move. Thomson was afraid that some of them might even die. By now these Africans knew how much more powerful their guns were than the Masai's weapons; yet they shook with fear. Thomson admits that he had to use a whip to make them go on.

Finally they approached the first Masai village. It contained about ten or twelve family kraal camps as well as the *manyatta* of the warriors. Thomson wrote that he saw a line of trees at the edge of an open plain. Columns of smoke were curling upward from the huts and cattle enclosures of the Masai. Each kraal camp was surrounded by a tall fence of thorns, with only one opening to it—its entrance. The explorers saw lines of cattle, guided by boys, old men, and their dogs, coming toward them on their way to pasture. The men and boys carried long spears and sticks.

Joseph Thomson's first encounter with the Masai was brief. He met a warrior, who was the leader, and presented him with gifts. The leader asked for more. Thomson was not an anthropologist. He had not studied closely the customs of African people and did not fully realize that it is a widespread custom to expect gifts from chiefs and from men of wealth. To the Masai, Thomson with all his trade goods and carriers was obviously a man of great riches. The Masai did not even think it necessary to thank a gift giver, since he had more than enough left for himself. This Thomson did not know, and he felt that the Masai were very greedy.

Thomson explained to them that he needed the rest of the things he carried to trade for food with other people, whom he expected to meet outside the boundaries of Masailand. The Masai did not understand this. The warriors, finding that Thomson could not be persuaded to give up the rest of his trade goods, began to threaten him. Thomson's carriers were trembling with fear. There seemed to be nothing to do but retreat. Under cover of darkness Thomson left the Masai warriors. He was glad to escape with whatever he had left of the baggage he had brought with him.

Yet many years later, Thomson found himself longing for the African wilderness. He told his friends that he would like to return to see once again the beautiful sunlit plains of the Masai.

TWO

GROWING UP

The Masai customs have much in common with those of other nomadic herders of Africa, but it is not easy to learn details of their personal life. These people are so independent and proud and so wary of strangers that they do not like to talk about themselves, for fear this knowledge might be used to change their ways. The Masai definitely want to avoid rapid change. Of all the Africans, this group has resisted modern customs the most. They live today almost as they lived a century ago.

It was fortunate, therefore, that a Scotsman, named A. C. Hollis, came to know a young African, called Ole Menye, who belonged to the Baraguyu, a tribe related to the Masai. During the famine of 1890 he ran away from home and ended up at a mission school in Chagaland. The missionaries gave the boy a Christian name, Justin Ole Menye, and were pleased that as he grew older he liked school.

At the beginning of the twentieth century A. C. Hollis was the Chief Secretary of the East Africa Protectorate Office. He learned the Masai language and grew to love the people. He decided to write a grammar of their language for English-speaking people, so his government might understand the Masai better. The friendly missionaries suggested that Hollis take Justin Ole Menye as an assistant, because the young man was very intelligent and was quick to grasp problems that were put to him. Hollis agreed.

The two men worked together on a book, which was not only about the Masai language, but included valuable information about the ways of the Masai—about marriage, childbirth, initiation of boys and girls, warriors and cattle raids, religion and prayers, myths, legends, and proverbs. These very personal details were known only to the Masai themselves.

The Masai are divided into two main groups: the farmers, the Arusha, and the herders, the Masai. The herders are further divided into four main clans. The first and foremost clan is called L'Aiser. It has been said that the tallest men come from this first clan, and all the powerful medicine men come from it. A medicine man, as a rule, hands down his knowledge for curing people, his knowledge of rain making, and his ability to foretell the future to his oldest son. In this way his skills remain within the same clan. If a man has no sons, he hands his information and his insignia of office to a close Aiser relation.

The other three clans call themselves Il-Mengana, Il-Mokesen, and Il-Molelyan. However, when the Aisers and Menganas went on raids, they called themselves Black Cattle. The Mokesens and Molelyans called themselves Red Bulls. These names carried a supernatural meaning. The Masai believed that raided cattle followed more readily those Masai warriors who were also named Cattle.

Each of the four clans is made up of several subclans. There are about twenty groups in all. These subclans also have names, such as the Scars, the Lion Killers, the Long-sighted Ones, and Flesh-on-the-ribs. The members of the clans and subclans differ in appearance, and other Masai can readily identify them. Each group dresses a bit differently and marks its cattle with distinct ear and skin brands. Not only can a Masai easily recognize the group to which a person belongs, but the neighboring people also know them, even from a distance, by their dress and by the marks that the warriors paint on their shields.

A Masai usually has more than one wife. Some-

times he has three, four, and five wives, if he is
the owner of a large herd of cattle. Several wives
are needed to help tend the herd and to milk the
cows. A man does not milk his cows. It is woman's
work.

A man divides his herd among his wives, so that
each woman and her children have a separate herd
of cattle, sheep, and goats to care for. The children grow up with their mother's herd. Each boy
knows every head of his mother's cattle and can
recognize it even if it is mixed with any other
herd. But neither a man nor a boy is willing to tell
just how many head of cattle, sheep, or goats are
in his herd. A Masai does not like to count the
exact number of cattle he has. He feels that such
boasting might bring bad luck to his cattle. Nor
does a man like to tell how many wives and children he has, for fear of bad luck. He is pleased to
have people know that he has large herds, a few
wives, and many sons, but he wants no one to count
them.

The rounded hut of a Masai family is a tiny,

dark, one-room dwelling, which the mother has built herself by placing sticks, interwoven with boughs, into the ground and tying them together at the top. She then plasters mud over the whole basketlike structure, which looks like an Eskimo igloo. This mud is mixed with fresh cow dung, which has an agreeable odor to the Masai since, from babyhood, they smell their cattle herded outside in the enclosure.

When it rains, the hut is protected further with a hide thrown over its flat roof. The entrance extends at right angles, resembling a narrow porch. The door is so low that a person almost has to crawl through it on all fours. Even inside, one cannot stand up comfortably.

The hut is meagerly furnished. The mother's bed is a bullock's skin placed either directly on the red earth floor or over a low base of dried grass and twigs. Two or three low stools and several gourds of different sizes occupy the rear of the hut. Also, a few extra skins and bags are stacked against the walls. There is a coarse clay cooking pot with handles, which the Masai women usually make themselves. They sometimes warm milk over a tiny fire inside the hut. Several small holes in the walls, close to the beds, allow smoke to escape and provide ventilation.

The Masai men offer prayers when there is a special occasion or a special need for supernatural help in a raid or war, or when the seasonal rains are slow in coming. But the women and children usually pray together twice a day. They pray at dawn to Venus, the morning star, chanting, "I pray you, who rises yonder, to hear me. Keep my cows alive. Take care of our people."

Soon after marriage a young wife begins to pray fervently for a child. Her prayer is a simple and direct chant, as she sprinkles milk from a gourd in the four directions. "Give me the offspring, you who brings thunder and rain. We pray to you every day."

Once she has given birth to a child the mother knows her prayers have been heard. Henceforth,

she will continue praying that she have more children and that they stay healthy. She will pray simply, "Guard my child," or "Guard my sons and daughters."

When the young mother was initiated into womanhood, an older woman taught her about childbirth and told her what to do after her baby was born. The girl also helped her mother and the other mothers in the household to care for their babies. So she is quite familiar with the routine of nursing and caring for her own child. She also knows a few simple remedies for stomach-aches and for rashes on the baby's skin, and how to help it with teething and minor ailments. Mostly she uses a few herbs and salves. For more serious ailments her husband will call in a medicine man.

A Masai child is born in its mother's small hut. An old woman, or one of its father's other wives, assists at the birth. Neither the father nor any other man is permitted near the hut. The father is told about the child later, and does not see it until a few days after its birth. Fathers, too, want many children, especially sons, because they are needed as herders and later as warriors.

The women of a kraal camp perform the ceremony that follows the birth of a child. As soon as they get the news that the child has been born, they gather together and come to the new mother's home. Each brings a small gourd of milk for her to drink. The few women who enter the hut fill it with talk and cries of praise, as they peer at the infant. To show their good will toward the child and its parents, they spit frequently because, in Masai beliefs, either water or spit helps remove any evil a person may think or speak. The women exchange comments and offer the mother the milk they have brought.

A sheep has been tied nearby to await the birth of the child. Now it is slaughtered and roasted outside the hut. When the meat is ready, two of the women bring it in. Each woman is invited to take a slice of the meat, which they call the Purifier, and eat it. The freshly killed and cooked

mutton is quite a treat for most of the women.
Each eats her portion quickly and begins to chant
a prayer of thanksgiving:

> Hail the day on which this child is born.
> Oh joy!
> Let us all sing and praise her
> That she gave birth to a son
> For whom she longed.
> Greet this day with joy.
> Our hearts are glad.

The next important event in the family's life
is naming the child. This time a bullock is slaughtered. The Masai call the bullock the Offspring,
in honor of the infant. For this important occasion, the father has selected a perfect black bullock—without a blemish. Such a bullock is permitted to have only a small white or brown spot
on it. Since the Masai love their cattle, to kill such
a perfect animal is indeed a fine way for a father
to honor his child.

The guests invited to the naming feast sit patiently around the fire while the meat is roasting. They fill the time by recalling naming ceremonies at which they were the parents and by telling how they raised their children. They exchange news about herds and reported cattle raids. The men may play a game with pebbles, which are rolled into holes in the ground.

When the meat is ready, the guests are called to come over and take slices of it. Among the Masai, men and women do not eat together. In fact, people prefer to eat without being watched by a crowd. Each person takes a chunk of meat and departs to eat it in his own home. Again the women bring small gourds of milk for the mother. They give her the milk, take the meat, and then depart.

The head of the Offspring bullock has been left by the door. The Masai usually throw heads and bones outside the thorn fence that encircles the kraal camp. But they save the head of an Offspring bullock and treat its hide in a special way. The tail is left on the hide, which is rolled up in the mother's hut. It will be tanned later.

That evening the mother places her infant on her back in a piece of kidskin or cloth and goes out to milk the cows. She returns to the hut with a gourd of milk. Three elders and the father have been sitting outside on stools waiting for her to return from the milking. They now come into the hut. While the mother holds the child, they speak the name they have decided on, such as Engipika,

Lesini, or Lemon-doi, if it is a boy, or Endebelai, Linde, Mone, or Beegi, if it is a girl.

For the next two years the child, whether it is a boy or a girl, remains close to its mother. The mother nurses the child whenever it cries, and the nursing usually lasts for two years. As the child begins teething, the mother occasionally gives it pieces of meat to chew. The Masai cattle are lean and tough, so chewing the meat is good exercise for the baby's teeth. However, some claim that the teeth of the Masai protrude, because youngsters have to pull so hard on the tough meat. They can't bite it the way we do, with our incisors, since their lower two incisors have been pulled.

All Masai pull out the two front teeth in the lower jaw. The mother pulls out a child's soon after they develop, and the medicine man pulls out a boy's second set during initiation. Europeans have tried to explain that this custom may have originated because the Masai used to get lockjaw frequently. They discovered that by having this permanent opening in their mouths, they could suck in food and drink milk and keep from starving to death. Now it is a custom, and the Masai are so used to having two lower front teeth missing that they think a person who has not had them pulled chews like a donkey. It makes the Masai laugh.

A Masai child is given anything it asks for. Wherever the mother goes, the child follows, either on her back or led by the hand. The Masai mother is not at all strict about child rearing. She permits her child to train itself over a few years, instead of teaching it early as European and American mothers do.

But the Masai mother does want her child to be beautiful. She mixes sheep's fat with red clay and rubs the child well with it, so its skin shines a golden brown. The mother also adds rounded weights to the child's ear lobes, so they will stretch until the lobes reach the shoulder. This is done for both boys and girls, and is considered very handsome.

Boys and girls enjoy a carefree early childhood —a life in the open with very few restrictions and little supervision. At the age of five a boy joins his brothers and other boys in the camp, and they play among the cattle. They come home for a drink of milk and blood, and are then free to return to their companions and games. When thirsty, a boy far from home puts his mouth directly under a cow's udders and takes a drink.

The games of these children are not very different from the outdoor games children play the world over. The boys play at being herders. They collect pebbles and sort them into cattle, sheep, and goats. Each boy names his cattle and scratches marks on the pebbles for cattle brands, so he can identify them. Sticks are their spears, clubs, and fire-making drills. They raid their playmates' pebble herds and return "home" with their raided cattle. The boys put berries on the pebbles and pierce them with a sharp twig, pretending they are getting blood from a bullock. Then they drink the berry juice.

Little girls build huts in the sand and surround them with thorn fences for the cattle. They have toy gourds for milking their cows, and stack them inside the huts. Their mothers help them make dolls out of bundles of grass or from the fruit of the sausage tree. They wrap the fruit in pieces of sheepskin or goatskin, and the dolls become baby boys and girls for the little girls to care for.

From the age of eight a boy is expected to help with the herd, but he enjoys the freedom to wander, if he so desires. Older boys can leave home for days at a time, unless they are needed to care for the herd. Very early they learn to be self-reliant, to know their way along the trails, and to use their small spears, which they hurl at buffalo and other wildlife on the grasslands. When the youngsters spear a wild animal, they carry away only its hide and horns. They leave the carcass for the ever-present lions, hyenas, and vultures to finish.

The boys like to play among the cattle, too. They play a game of raiding cattle. One boy selects a cow while the others hide. When he is ready and calls them, the boys rush out from several direc-

tions and pretend they are an enemy who has come to raid the herd. The boy fights them off with his stick. A boy touched by the stick is considered killed and drops out of the game. Those who manage to evade the stick and touch the cow are safe. These games are an excellent preparation for their future life as warriors on the open plains.

The boys also play the game with pebbles, which they roll into shallow holes in the ground. The pebble game holds their attention for a long time. Even warriors and old men find the pebble game interesting and an exciting challenge to their skill.

Since Masailand is in the tropics, the children learn early not to get overheated during their games. They develop a slow, gliding, steady walk that can carry them long distances but, at the same time, does not overheat them as would racing and jumping.

A Masai husband visits each wife's hut on certain days. On the days when Father is to come, special preparations are made for him. Some of the older boys and girls may be away preparing for their initiation ceremonies. Those remaining at home are rubbed with fresh coats of grease. The mother may have her head shaved by an older woman in the camp, since it is not becoming for a woman to have hair on her head.

When the father's visiting day comes, he may be returning after a long absence. He may have been away trading, and the family looks forward to gifts. He may bring a few extra head of cattle, perhaps some more jewelry for his wife, perhaps a new spear he had a smith make for his son. Everyone likes to receive gifts, and the family show their delight and surprise, but no one says thank-you to the father, because it is not customary. As an additional treat, the father will draw fresh blood from a bullock in the kraal. Since a family does not eat together, father and sons will enjoy the drink of fresh blood. The mother and daughters of the household wait until the men drink before they take the gourd of blood and drink.

A family does not stay in the hut, since it is so dark and crowded. They sit outside and enjoy the sunset and the cool breeze that comes with evening on the high plains. They watch their cattle and talk about the condition of the pasture, the need for rain, the help the children have been giving with the herding. The father looks over the young animals and is pleased that they are growing. He knows that his wife has been letting the cows give ample milk to their calves, and is not taking too much away for her own children and herself. It is understandable to the mother that the father should be as much concerned about the cattle's welfare as he is about his children's.

Boys from the age of thirteen to seventeen are ready for initiation and circumcision. The initiation ceremonies for Masai youngsters are quite complicated, because of the way they count the years that lead up to initiation and the way they set the periods of initiation for groups of youngsters.

Boys from several kraal camps, who are ready for initiation, gather near a medicine man's camp. Only those who live very far away from the medicine man are allowed to bring their spears. Most have left them at home. They merely bring their fire-making sticks and their clubs, which are tucked in their belts.

The medicine man looks them over and separates them into two groups, called age sets. The boys who look bigger will be initiated and circumcised first, and the medicine man places them in the right-hand group. They might be circumcised, for example, in January of 1963. The smaller boys belong to the left-hand group. They will have to wait for another three-and-a-half years to be circumcised—June of 1966. Together, the right-hand group and the left-hand group are called one age set, and all these youngsters are expected to feel a loyalty to one another. Throughout life they will be ready to help one another, because they belong to the same age set.

The boys in the left-hand group leave immediately for their homes. The boys in the right-hand group remain. Each boy's father has sent along some bullocks and a milch cow, so his son will have food and also something to share with his new friends. They paint their bodies white with chalk and settle down for two or three months to learn their duties as future warriors.

As is the custom among warriors, the boys select a spokesman from among themselves—a leader—who will speak for them when the need arises. Sitting day after day in the shade of the kraal amidst the smell of the cattle, they listen as the medicine men and elders tell them about the ways of their people.

A boy is circumcised three months later, after he returns home. The operation is performed, not by Masai men, but by the Dorobo, the hunters who live on Masai lands. The boy's father invites the Dorobo men to perform the operation on his son and pays for it with a bullock or a sheep. Cattle are always tied in with all ceremonies. The boy's father kills a bullock in his son's honor and names it Animal-to-be-taken-out. This means that the boy has been taken out of the ranks of boys and has become a young warrior. His sisters plant a special tree in front of his hut.

Before the boy is circumcised, his head is shaved. He washes himself in water in which a special herb that lessens the pain has been soaked. He then lies down on a skin in front of the hut and awaits the Dorobo men. One man holds the boy, and the other performs the circumcision. Even though the boy's parents, the elders, and the medicine men have instructed him not to wince or make a sound during the painful ordeal, there is always the fear that he will cry out. So his parents go away and hide themselves during the operation. If the boy cries out, people will come looking for his mother to punish her for raising a coward.

After circumcision, a boy remains inside the hut for several days. When he is able to walk, he puts on a long blanketlike garment and carries special bows and arrows that the men of the camp have made for him. With these he shoots at all the young girls he meets. The arrows are blunt and do not hurt anyone, and they mark the beginning of his interest in girls, which is approved by everyone.

With shaved heads and long garments, these boys could be mistaken for girls. To avoid embarrassment, they paint their faces with chalk when they go out. After his initiation a boy lets his hair grow. He will be able to plait it, warrior

fashion, by the time he gets into the ranks of junior warriors.

Now the boys enjoy a period of total freedom from herding. They merely wait for the second initiation, when they will become junior warriors. During this time they wander about in bands all over the country, living on their own and familiarizing themselves with their lands, with other Masai who live on these lands, and with the farming Arusha.

When the initiation ceremony for junior war-

riors takes place, the boys move to special bachelor
huts, called *manyattas*. A *manyatta* is a warriors'
village. It is made up of clusters of huts, specially
built to house warriors. But unlike the kraal camps
of the Masai, a *manyatta* has no thorn fence sur-
rounding it, and the warriors must take turns
guarding it day and night against wild animals and
raiders. Each cluster of a dozen or so kraal camps
will have in the vicinity a *manyatta* to which the
people look for protection. The kraal camps move
to fresh ground every six or eight months, but the
manyatta remains relatively permanent for two or
three years.

During these years junior warriors practice
with spears and war clubs, and train for defense
and attack. In the past they went on raids periodically and thus increased their fathers' wealth.
Some, unfortunately, also met with death, and so
their careers were cut short. Today, on the whole,
the Masai warriors enjoy a life of ease and freedom in the wild outdoors.

The Masai girls have an initiation, too, when

they reach fourteen or fifteen. Like the boys before initiation, the girls go off to live by themselves away from their mothers. Their huts are supervised by old women, who teach them about housekeeping, marriage, and caring for babies. No men are allowed near the huts where the girls live. Soon after her initiation (puberty) ceremony a girl is ready for marriage, but a boy has to wait for a few years before he can marry.

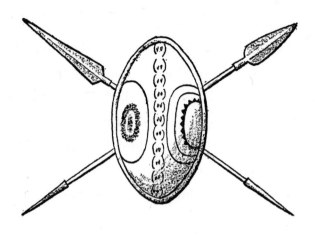

THREE

WARRIORS

The picturesque Masai warrior is known not only to the large African world, but also in Europe, Asia, and the Americas. To his people, he is *olmurran*, protector of the cattle. He is pictured standing, still as a bronze statue, long-legged and almost naked, with one long, lean arm resting on a spear. The belt around his slim waist holds a fierce curved sword. The small square of kidskin thrown over his shoulders leaves his body free for its graceful, pliant movements. His long, thin face, with high cheekbones and narrow eyes, is set proudly on a long neck. The warrior's eyes are bright, curious. He is poised at all times, and does not look away when someone stares at him. He returns the gaze directly. You look at him, and he looks right back at you, full of dignity and self-confidence.

Once a young man has attained the rank of warrior, he looks forward to some fifteen years of adventurous life. Four to five years of this time will be spent in a separate home with his own age set. When warriors meet, one group shouts "Entasupai!" The other replies, "Hepa!" These words are the equivalents of our hello. The men stop and face one another. They thrust their long spears into the ground, lean against the dark walls of their huts, and touch hands. "Do you bring good news?" they ask. The newcomers reply, "Good news only." The men crowd together. When they tire of standing on one leg, they cross their long limbs and, standing on both feet, sway gracefully from side to side. Or they sit down on the ground, their knees drawn up against their chins. Their small kidskin or cloth capes cover them entirely and comfortably, as would blankets. In this position warriors sit through an entire afternoon, talking, gossiping, laughing, playing endless games with pebbles.

The Masai have been called graceful and fluent talkers. When a warrior has something important to say, he raises his voice to gain attention. The rest quiet down and listen to him. As a device to help his memory, a speaker holds in his hand a few twigs. As he finishes a point in his speech, he drops one twig. When he has none left in his hand, the speech is finished and the speaker sits down.

When the news reaches the warriors that a neighboring group has accumulated a large herd of cattle, they begin to plan a raid. But first they must gather a larger force of men. The warriors are sure that their age mates in the nearby *manyattas* will be glad to join them.

The self-reliant Masai have no regular chiefs who inherit their position. Each age set of warriors selects a spokesman. The spokesman, or leader, to be selected must be handsome, tall, and strong. That he is fearless goes without saying. The men must all be brave to reach the rank of warrior. But often, because they live in a hot climate, a man's eyesight is not good. A leader's eyes must be perfect and must not be discolored. Nor can any man be a leader who has previously killed a person. He must be a warrior without blemish—like a perfect bull.

A few warriors usually decide among themselves on the man who is to be selected as spokesman. They also tell their choice to the medicine man, so he can approve of it. Each warrior knows how much he himself wishes to avoid this grave responsibility. They, therefore, never tell the warrior or even hint to him that he has been selected. They feel sure that were they to tell him, he would immediately run away and kill somebody, just to get out of taking this office. Therefore, the choice is kept secret, so much so that the chosen warrior, along with the others, even helps select the special cloth for the mantle and the pair of special long earrings, called *surutya*, they plan to give him when he is nominated. The *surutya* may be worn only by men who have distinguished themselves or who are the wealthy owners of herds.

The warriors now build a special hut for the leader. Again, the unsuspecting warrior helps his companions in all these activities. Perhaps, as he works, the others exchange sly glances. They can almost see him struggling to escape when he hears the news that he has been chosen.

The warriors finish the hut and bring over a few of their best milch cows for the new leader. All is now complete. Again, they gather for a chat. When the unsuspecting warrior arrives to join his companions and plunges his spear into the ground, they seize him and pin down his arms and legs. He struggles in vain, for he is alone and outnumbered. The men throw the new mantle over his shoulders and fasten the earrings on him. "Ho, to our olaigwenani, our spokesman!" they shout.

On the following day a dramatic raid is enacted. A black bullock with a white neck and belly is brought to the leader's hut. The warriors immediately surround the bullock in the same way they plan to encircle a herd during the raiding. Two men hold the bullock, while a third stabs it in the nape of its neck—as all cattle are slaughtered. The carcass is then skinned on the spot. Thus the warriors will slaughter some of the raided cattle.

Next the warriors build a fire and throw a buffalo horn into it. When the fire begins to die down, the warriors race to get the horn. This is like rushing into the heat of battle. The one who reaches the fire first thrusts his hand into the hot coals and picks up the smoldering horn. He holds it aloft, crying triumphantly, "I have finished it."

This ends the ceremony of selecting a spokesman. The raid will be successful.

The Masai do not like to work with iron, and

have beliefs and customs that forbid making iron
weapons and tools. Perhaps in the early days they
obtained iron from the earth and hammered their
own weapons, but for the past few centuries they
have come to depend entirely on their smiths for
all the metal they need. These smiths belong to a
separate group of Masai. In the past each clan had
its smiths, and every settlement had a few who
lived nearby.

The Masai call their smiths Kunono. All the
Kunono belong to one clan, the Kipuyoni. The
language the smiths speak is related to that of the
Masai, but the warriors say it is hard for them to
understand it. The Kipuyoni clan keeps to itself.
They pass on their skills in ironworking from
father to son and do not intermarry with the other
Masai clans. The smiths are a poor people. Their
huts are even darker and more humble than those
of the other Masai. Evidently they have very few
cattle. It is believed—and the Masai themselves
continue to spread these beliefs—that the smiths

have no luck with cattle raising. Cattle are supposed to die in the smiths' kraals.

The Masai fear the smiths to some extent, because they work with iron and fire, and so they speak of them as powerful but unclean. At best a warrior's visit to a smithy is hurried. The warrior orders what he needs and returns at a time agreed upon to get the finished weapon. Before he touches it, the warrior rubs his hands with grease and then rubs the weapon with it. He will not touch, unpro-

tected by a coat of grease, the hand of the smith or anything the smith has touched. After a man has examined and accepted the weapon the smith has made, he usually leaves a scrawny sheep, bullock, or goat in trade for it. There is no bargaining, since the warrior is the stronger. The smith depends entirely upon the warrior's generosity. However, in the behavior of the Masai, one is not generous with an inferior. Generosity extends only to one's own family, to clan members, and to one's age set. So the reason the smiths have no luck with their cattle may be because they get the very poorest animals in trade.

A smith gets iron from secret places in Masailand, or he trades for it with the coastal people. He also speaks Swahili, which is necessary for trading with these people. A stone anvil, a leather bellows, a pair of pincers, and a hammer are his simple tools. With these, a Masai smith, who is really a fine craftsman, makes magnificent shovel-sized spears, hatchets, knives, swords, needles, bracelets, anklets, and copper-wire coils for chest, arm, leg, and ear ornaments. The smiths also make cowbells, which the herders attach to the leading cows or bulls.

The warrior's shield is his proud possession. It is oval in shape and made of tough hide, an excellent protection for his almost naked body. The shields are colored white, red, black, and gray. The white comes from white clay. The red comes from blood, mixed with the juice of berries. Black is obtained from the ashes of certain plants and from charred potsherds (broken pottery) and gourds. Gray is used more rarely and is obtained from crushed cinders. Each shield bears a special design, which is familiar both to other Masai and to their enemies. The Masai know from the markings on the shields to which subclan and age set a warrior belongs. Additional markings distinguish the bearer as a very brave man, who has shown valor in raids and battles and who has killed a number of men.

The Masai warriors make themselves ready

with the help of the medicine men who, they believe, can foretell whether a raid will be successful. Added to the prayers and chants of the medicine men are their own and those of their women. The warriors' families pray to the Black God and to the morning star. No man dares to refuse a request when a person who carries a bunch of grass and a gourd of milk comes to plead or pray. So the Masai tie grass to their clothing and sprinkle milk from gourds as offerings to the god for his good will, hoping the god will not refuse them either. They pray to triumph over the enemy. They pray that the enemy's power will be broken, that his property be burned and his cattle safely brought to the Masai *manyattas*. The women pray that their sons and husbands may return safely from the successful battle.

After a last leap of their war dance, the warriors depart in the midst of dances and grass waving by the women, who also sprinkle them with milk from gourds. The old men make their farewells by sprinkling milk and honey wine on the ground.

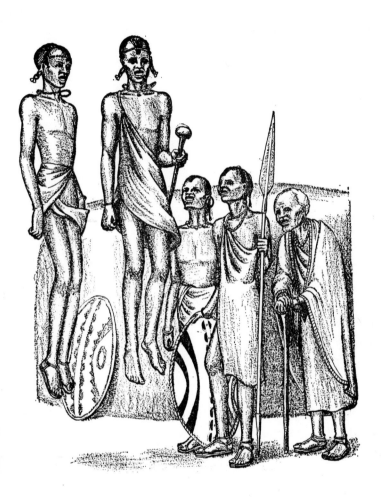

For several days before going on a raid the warriors have feasted on freshly killed and roasted meat to tide them over the strenuous days ahead. The medicine men have mixed the contents of a bullock's stomach with a special bark and roots. This the warriors drink to gain more courage and strength. While on the march, when the warriors are near exhaustion, they mix more of this drink to quench their thirst and to give them further strength. They also mix the crushed bark of another tree in water and drink it. This mixture turns red, and the warriors feel that they will gain courage from it, since it looks like blood.

Warriors are not permitted to smoke or to drink the Masai honey wine or beer. They cannot mix milk and meat. Before the warriors eat meat they take an herb mixture that makes them vomit, so they are sure that all the milk they had in them is gone before they touch the meat.

Thomson, who resented the boldness of the Masai, described the warriors as "young, bloated cutthroats on the march."

When the warriors reach enemy country, they plant their spears in the ground. Each announces himself proudly. "I am the son of Lesini. Whether I conquer or die, it will be in this place."

The warriors chant prayers for a successful raid. "Bless our spears," they pray. "And may we bring home large herds. Make this raid better than all past raids."

The enemy, seeing a large number of warriors on the march, sometimes abandon their homes and turn to flight, driving their cattle before them. The Masai warriors set fire to the enemy's homes and race to overtake those who have escaped. The cattle, frightened and confused by the fires, start a stampede. The warriors usually try to kill or capture the enemy's camp leader. Once a leader is killed, the enemies lose heart. They will abandon their cattle and run for their lives. The same is true of the Masai. Once their leader is killed they, too, give up and go home. Their leader is like their heart. The medicine man has given him magical powers. If he is killed, they stop the fight, believing that the enemy has a stronger power, which they cannot overcome. So the brave warriors turn back.

A war is fought differently from a raid. In war there is no sudden attack as in a raid for cattle. Instead, elders from both sides meet first to discuss the differences that have arisen in disputes over grazing lands, water rights, or even raids. When they are unable to settle the argument peacefully, the enemies set a day for a battle and agree on a place to fight. Both sides then get together on the battlefield and declare a temporary truce, while the women build huts and set up housekeeping. The fighting that takes place is in the open, with the elders and the women and children on both sides cheering and praying for their kin. The winners of the battle receive the cattle of the enemy and may even drive the enemy out of the lands they have lived in.

Fighting does not end with a successful war or raid. Excited and flushed with triumph, the warriors return to their homes and set about to divide the spoils. A certain number of cattle is set aside by custom for the medicine man or men, who prayed for the success of the war or raid and predicted that the Masai would win. The warriors hold contests to decide who gets the remaining cattle. So the final division of spoils depends on the strength and endurance of the warriors. The strongest gets the most. If a warrior can hold his own for three days in single combat against all comers, the remaining cattle are his. To kill a man during such a contest is not considered a crime. His relatives will not try to avenge him. No one avenges a warrior who is weak and unable to save his own life in a fair fight. Only if a man is murdered treacherously without warning do his age set and kinsmen seek revenge. For such a crime the elders usually rule a payment of forty-nine bullocks. The murderer's kinsmen pay the fine out of their herds.

A warrior who is the oldest son in a family gives all the cattle he has gained in a raid to his father. He does not keep any for himself. But a younger son is allowed to keep the cattle he has won in a raid. His mother and still younger brothers and sisters will care for them while he is living away from home. In a way, this equalizes the effect of the inheritance customs among the Masai. Upon his father's death, the oldest son receives the largest share of his father's herds. The younger brothers do not inherit as many cattle. It is up to the oldest brother to give them a share of his newly acquired herds. The custom of keeping the cattle they have raided helps younger brothers acquire larger herds of their own.

If a warrior has been wounded in battle and feels that he will not survive, he begs his closest friend in his age set to finish his suffering with the thrust of a spear. A friend is bound to obey such a request. However, the Masai have some knowledge of curing their wounded. They do not allow wounded men to have milk, but give them a special herb drink that quenches their thirst and has curing power. If a warrior's arm or leg has been broken, his friends open up the flesh and bring the edges of the bone together. Then they stitch the wound with sinew from the back of an ox and bind the limb in a piece of kidskin. Eventually the bone may heal. The Masai remove broken ribs entirely and insert in their place new ribs from a freshly killed sheep. They pour sheep's fat into the wound and sew it up. They also perform a similar operation on a man who is speared in the abdomen. They replace his intestines, stuff sheep's fat into the wound, and sew it up with sinew.

The Masai say they can amputate limbs successfully. Many Masai who claim skill at surgery learned by practicing on cattle. After curing cows, bulls, sheep, and goats, they feel they can operate on wounded warriors. We do not know how successful these operations are. Certainly our surgeons would despair at such procedures.

A clan of pastoral Masai once made a solemn and lasting peace with the Arusha farmers. The elders of the Arusha met with two elders of the herders. Each group brought along a cow, a calf, and a woman with a baby. With great ceremony and dignity, while the people on both sides watched, the herders gave their cow and calf to the Arusha and received in turn the Arusha's cow and calf. Then the Arusha child was taken by the pastoral Masai mother and nursed, while her own baby was nursed by the Arusha mother. This exchange created a permanent truce between the two groups. The assembled people on both sides cheered and waved bundles of grass, to show that they all agreed to peace.

If the Masai do not want to make a lasting agreement, they merely enter into a blood brotherhood. A Masai elder sits down next to an elder from the enemy camp. Each makes a small cut in his left arm and lets his blood drip on some freshly roasted meat, which he eats. This ceremony creates a temporary peace.

However, in periods of drought or when there is sickness in the camps or an epidemic strikes the herds, the warriors are so busy helping their people that raids and quarrels have to wait. Helping the people is a warrior's first duty. Warriors will work all day to exhaustion, lifting the heavy leather buckets out of the deep wells to water the stock and to fill the women's gourds with water for the camps. Wherever help is needed, the people can rely on the strength and support of their *ilmurran*, the protectors of the cattle.

FOUR

LIVING TOGETHER

The life of a warrior whose father has died, making him head of the household, changes overnight. He gives up his enjoyable life in the *manyatta* and becomes a settled man with responsibilities. He has to manage a large household, made up of old men and women, his father's widows, and all his brothers and sisters, whether they are married or not. Good management is essential if the new head of the household is to keep up the herds he inherited, if he is to keep a large family fed and at peace and harmony with one another, and if he is to earn respect in the camp. It goes without saying that he also wants to enlarge the herds his father left him and to assure them good pasture. The new head of a household tries to be very fair. He frequently consults with the elders in his family, who have greater experience and wisdom. He also asks the advice of other elders in the camp, listening closely and respectfully to their words and warnings.

The widows usually keep the cattle allotted them by their husband during his lifetime and pass them on to their adult sons. If the father had any brothers, the eldest son of the family asks them to marry the widows whose children are too young to take over the cattle. The wives take their milch cows and herd with them when they go to live in their second husband's kraal camp. They also take their young children with them. Men are very glad to marry widows, for they not only get good herds of cattle, but also children who, as they get older, will help take care of both their mother's and their new father's cattle.

Usually the new head of the family has met a girl in the *manyatta*, who attracted him and whom he now wants to marry. Masai girls are very pretty, slender, and graceful, with high cheekbones and dark, shiny eyes, narrow with an upward slant. A girl does not marry unless she wishes to and unless she likes the groom. If she does like him, she says so, without any of the shyness that we might expect of young girls.

Having made his choice and learned that the girl likes him too, the warrior goes to her parents' camp and brings a small gift of tobacco for her father. Sometimes, even if the girl has been initiated, her parents may feel that she is still too young to marry and leave her mother. Although they know that the girl likes the man, they beg him to wait a little, and the warrior agrees. He may, in the meantime, court another girl, too. But he keeps on visiting the first girl's parents and continues to bring them small gifts of tobacco, honey for the household, or perhaps some grain and vegetables he has received for a sheep or a goat.

The girl is pleased with the visits. She is usually on the lookout for the man's coming, her head neatly shaved and her one-piece, wrap-around skirt carefully tied. She wears chain earrings and bead necklaces, and rubs herself with an extra coat of grease to make her skin shine. Both young men and women rub themselves all over with crushed aromatic plants, so they will smell nice. In order to appear more attractive, a girl gathers leaves at the water's edge and puts them into her ear lobes. She wears garlands of flowers. She also brings in aromatic plants and roots to decorate the hut. The Masai like to put aromatic plants on their beds, too.

A girl, like all Masai, brushes her teeth diligently with a toothbrush made from the fibers of a hibiscus bush, so her smile will be bright when her future husband comes to call. She greets him with a wide smile and shiny dark eyes. But although she would not like to remain unmarried for the rest of her life, she is in no hurry for an early marriage. She prefers to go about with her girl friends, visiting the *manyatta*. There the young people dance and sing nightly when the warriors are at home. To a Masai girl, marriage means caring for her children and for her husband's herd and milch cows. She feeds her children and her husband, too, when he comes to her hut. She has to keep the hut in good repair and build a new one every six or eight months when they move to new pasture.

A Masai woman does not work as hard, however, as her Arusha sisters. An Arusha woman works in the hot fields wielding a heavy hoe. Her small child is always with her—an extra weight. In most of Africa women toil in the fields and carry the heavy loads. The care and feeding of their children is their responsibility. The menfolk protect the family and teach their sons to do the same.

Even though parents prefer to have boys—

future herders and warriors—girls are appreciated too, because they help in the household with the milking and the babies. According to custom, the parents of a marriageable girl receive a gift of four head of cattle from her future husband, to make up for the loss of a daughter. One of these must be a milch cow with a calf. This gift the people call bride wealth. It is more correct to use the term *bride wealth* than *bride price*, since a girl is not bought by her husband. She marries a man, because that is what she wishes.

The groom brings the bride wealth with him when he and his family come to call upon the bride and take her to their camp. If the father-in-law asks for more bullocks, the groom will bring them to him. But this is understood to be a loan. The father-in-law will eventually pay it back. However, it establishes a cordial relationship between son-in-law and father-in-law.

When the guests assemble for the marriage feast, they are given meat, provided by the father of the bride. After the feast the bride and groom leave together for the new hut, which has been built for the bride.

The Masai prefer to hold their simple marriage ceremony after the calving season, because then the cows have abundant milk. Honeymoon couples drink a great deal of milk and eat vegetable food. The young husband, who was not allowed to smoke or take snuff while he was a warrior, is now permitted to do both. He may have inherited from his father fancy tobacco boxes and snuff-boxes, made of either ivory or horn. These boxes are not made by the Masai, but by some of their neighbors, especially the Dorobo. The Masai trade cattle for the boxes, because they value beautiful, artistic things.

An interesting custom calls for a warrior's wearing for a while the garment his wife wore as a girl, which she has now discarded. She dresses in the two-piece garment of a married woman. In the past this was made of leather and covered her from neck to ankles. Today the Masai women wear cotton clothing more and more. So their garments are usually two pieces of cotton cloth. One piece is a wrap-around skirt. The other is cut in the center, fits over her head, and hangs loosely to her middle.

Now, too, she gets the jewelry befitting a married woman, who always wears all the jewelry she owns. She does not like to take it off even when her husband is away from home. She would be very embarrassed to be seen without it and feels less attractive without her ornaments.

A woman wears circles of iron and copper wire that cover her neck and entire chest. Several earrings hang from her long, shoulder-length lobes. Her arms, forearms, and legs are covered with copper wire too. These ornaments are heavy. Some say they weigh as much as thirty pounds.

Fully dressed, either barefoot or wearing buffalo-hide sandals, Masai women must find it hard to move about under the weight of all that jewelry and wire. But they feel that this is very beautiful, and walk with a swaying, mincing step that makes the weight easier to carry. Women rub their legs and arms with grease and insert special leaves to soothe and cool the skin under the ornaments. When they move camp, it is probably quite wearying to walk long distances, carrying a baby and additional bundles. Yet they manage to run when there is danger.

A young married woman immediately takes on the household tasks that will be hers for the rest of her life. She tends the herd and the milch cows her husband has assigned to her. Later her children will help her. She makes a few new clay pots, collects a few gourds by trading extra milk for them with people in her camp or with farming visitors. When she is free, a woman visits other women in the camp. There is ample time for gossip, for village ceremonies, and for prayers. A woman observes the customs of her husband's camp and gets to know everyone. She does not, however, feel completely at home among her husband's people until her first child is born.

When the camp has to move to new grazing grounds a wife quickly packs her few possessions,

loads a donkey or donkeys, and is ready to move. The women carry the fire with them, if the distance they have to travel is short. If the destination is far away, they let the fire go out. Men start a new fire after the camp has settled in the new place.

To make a fire, a man places a flat piece of wood over a base of donkey's dung or dry grass. He then twirls a hard, pointed stick in a groove in the flat piece of wood, and the grass underneath is ignited. All the women rush out to light chips of wood, so they can start their own cooking fires and roast some meat or make a stew.

It takes only a short time for the women to build new huts, and life is again resumed as in the old camp. Since the huts are so small and dark and the outdoors is always warm and pleasant in the shade, even if dusty, a family spends most of its waking time outside the hut. There the very small children play, while the mother does her housework— tanning a skin, plaiting the unruly hair of a child, or making pots and scraping gourds. Her baby is always with her.

A man's second wife has her hut next door, and she, too, works outside with her children. If their herds are small, the two women may combine them under the guidance of one or two of their children. Helping one another is also part of family life when a man has more than one wife. Wives show jealousy of each other, too. They quarrel; later, they make up.

Although there are more boys born than girls, the Masai feel that polygamy—having more than one wife—is the best form of marriage. One reason, the elders say, is that no woman need stay unmarried. Many young men used to be killed on raids. Their sweethearts then married other warriors, even though they became second and third wives. The first wife always has more authority and rules over the ones who come after her. Her son is the first-born. He inherits the herds and becomes the male head of the family.

Although a man respects his father's other wives and wishes to be fair, it is only natural that he should favor his own mother—whom he loves—over anyone else. Custom also has it that a man should do everything to please his mother. So, as head of the family, he listens to her first. However, if the other women feel he is not fair, they can complain to their own fathers and brothers. A woman's kin will always fight her battles. Her father and brothers, painted and armed, come to the kraal camp. They begin their talks with the head of the family first. If they feel he is unwilling to give in, the father and brothers appeal to the camp council of elders for justice.

So the other wives are treated well, too. In fact, no one in a Masai camp feels that his life could be bettered. They are happy to follow the ways of their fathers.

When a man grows older and his sons reach the age of initiation, he, too, has to go through a ceremony. This ceremony is called "passing the fence." It really means that the father has to leave the rank of warriors and become an elder. No man is happy to join the rank of elders, even though they are highly respected. A man feels then that his life is ebbing, and his entire attitude changes from that of an active warrior to that of a patient elder. He becomes more kindly and more friendly. To a warrior every stranger is an enemy with whom he wishes to compete, but elders have been known to welcome strangers into their huts and to care for them when they were sick.

The elders of a camp might sit all day in front of their huts, smoke their pipes, and carry on endless discussions about everything around them, both natural and supernatural. They tell stories to youngsters and give young people advice out of the wisdom of experience. They hold councils, judge offenders, and see that the Masai ways and customs are observed and respected by everyone.

A father who is about to enter the rank of elders begins by preparing some honey-wine brew in a special hut away from his home. He remains there alone for four days and seldom leaves the hut, since his wives take turns bringing him food. He is allowed to leave only in an emergency, such as sickness at home or in the herds.

On the fourth day the father greases his body and is helped into a warrior's dress: a kidskin cap, a handsome tall headdress of ostrich feathers, a cape of vulture feathers, and anklets made of Colobus-monkey skins. If he is a man of wealth, he also puts on an ivory arm bracelet or a horn arm clamp. He fits his war club and knife into a belt of goat-

skin, picks up his spear and shield, and awaits the
elders. Together, carrying the gourds of honey
wine, they return to his home and pause by the
entrance. The elders then say, "Go, become an old
man." But the father protests and shouts, "Ho. I
shall not." This is repeated four times. On the
fifth count, as the elders say, "Go, become an old
man," the father meekly replies, "Ho. I have gone
then. I shall become an old man."

They enter the hut, and the father takes off his warrior's dress and puts on an ankle-length piece of skin or cloth—the dress of old people. Henceforth, the people of the camp will address him, not by his own name, but as "The-father-of-Engipika," or whatever his son's name is. Having turned into an elder, the father replies to the new name with a blessing for his son or sons, saying, "Herds and flocks." He means, "May my son have numerous herds and flocks." Again, as is the custom, the old men repeat "Father-of-Engipika" four times, and the father replies four times, "Herds and flocks." The ceremony is over. The new elder's sons may now be initiated.

All of the people's activities are regulated by customs, which children learn at home or by watching the adults of their camp. Because of this, Masai children, as well as adults, show perfect poise. They know what to expect of everyone in their camp. They know how other Masai and African visitors to their camp will behave and how they will speak.

Old people greet each other with, "Entasupai, oh elder," or "Entasupai, oh husband." Elders greet warriors with the query, "Friend?" When the warriors say yes, the elders reply, "Entasupai." The warriors say, "Hepa." The elders, to show good will toward the warriors, then spit into the palms of their hands before taking the warriors' hands.

Old men greet a woman with, "Entakwenya, oh wife." In return to this greeting, the woman merely makes a sound of recognition that sounds like "Igho."

It would be disrespectful for warriors to say, "Entakwenya, oh wife" when they meet a woman. A warrior says instead, "Entakwenya, oh lady." The woman replies with the same "Igho" sound. However, a warrior will greet young girls with "Entasupai, oh girls." And the girls reply gaily, "Hepa." This is a more friendly greeting than "Igho."

A boy could never presume to expect an elder or a warrior to take his hand in greeting. Instead, when an elder greets him, the boy lowers his head and presses it against the elder's stomach. Older women kiss children when they meet them. A child that has been thus kissed presses its face against the woman's chest.

Married women greet one another as, "Entakwenya, oh great lady." The reply to this is also "Igho." They greet warriors as well as boys with, "Entakwenya, oh child."

A warrior may greet his sister, too, very informally with, "Supai." She replies, "Hepa." When young people, whether boys or girls, meet one another, they say, "Takwenya!" If they are close relatives, they also kiss.

When a person is about to leave, his host says, "Good-by. Pray to God that you meet nobody but blind people, who will not harm you." The guest's reply is a good wish for the host. He says, "Lie down with honey and milk." The host replies, "So be it."

FIVE

MASAI BELIEFS

The pride and assurance of the Masai stem largely from their beliefs. Some people have said that the Masai have two gods: a Black God and a Red God. The Black God is good; the Red God is full of malice. Actually, the Masai believe in only one god, Enkai. Enkai is spoken of as the Black God when he answers his people's prayers by sending them rain and tall grass. When rain is withheld and the grass on the pastures has dried in the sun, Enkai is called the Red God.

In dry weather, when all the grass has been eaten, people begin to worry about their herds. The medicine men, the rain-makers, stop plucking their beards. The elders in the camps light fires of special wood, and the medicine men throw charms, which are called Ol-okora, into the fires. The women fasten grass to their clothes. All circle the fires and chant, "Black God, ho. God, water us. God of the rain cloud, quench our thirst." The women chant, "Bring rain and make the grass grow. Come, rain, and bring us fresh milk. . . ."

Such ceremonies may take place throughout the year. Like our own, the Masai year has twelve months, which are named for the type of weather each brings.

June is the first month of the year and the first month of the dry season. It follows the waning of the Pleiades in the sky. The Pleiades are said to bring rain.

July is the second month, and is also known as

the month of quarrels. Due to the drought, the women do not get enough milk from their cows, and they are tense and touchy, because their children are hungry.

August is the dry-grass month. People move their cattle to lower valleys, where moisture stays longer than in the higher elevations and where there is still some grass.

September is the month of hunger. Everything is dry.

October is called the last month of hunger. Rain is expected at its end.

November is the month of the white clouds— rain-bringing clouds.

December is the month of showers, and the ground is covered with little pools.

January is the month of lesser rain.

February is a month of still less rain. But the air is damp and brings insects. They attract birds, which perch on the cattle and feast on the insects in their hides.

March is the month of plenty. Black clouds

cover the skies. Heavy rain begins, and a deep mist hangs over the grasslands.

In April the rain continues. The bulls, well fed now, get restless, and the herders tie them up in the enclosures to keep them from running away.

In May the Pleiades—the rain bringers—set. This is the end of the year, the end of the wet season.

Since there are thirteen lunar months in the year, the twelve-month calendar of the Masai is not exact. If it continues to rain in June, they say they've made a mistake. "It must still be May if it is raining." Later, if December continues as hot as November, they say, "This must still be November, the month of white, rain-bringing clouds."

Although the Masai speak of four seasons, there is actually little difference among them. It is usually hot and dry during the day, but the nights are cooler. When it rains everything gets soaked. The red clayey African soil tends to pack,

and the paths in the kraal camps become slippery
and are covered with pools of water. There is fog
and humidity. The huts leak, even though they
are covered with hides. The people's clothing does
not dry. The body feels damp, and the insects and
mosquitoes feast on men and cattle. It could be a
depressing period, but the Masai know that the
weather is bringing new grass for their beloved
herds. There is now ample water in the water holes
and streams. Men and cattle can drink their fill.
This makes the personal discomfort easier to bear.

The Masai believe that their god and the sun
and the moon follow a way of life similar to their
own. The sun and moon are married. The sun is
the husband; the moon, the wife. One day they
quarreled. The moon struck the sun on the head.
The sun hit back and damaged the moon's face.
When the sun looked at itself and noticed that its
face was badly battered, it felt ashamed. In order
to hide it from the eyes of human beings, who

looked daily at the sun, it turned on a very bright light. To this day the sun dazzles the eyes. People have to turn their faces away from it and do not see its battered face. Not so the moon. She is not ashamed to let people see that her mouth is swollen and crooked and that one of her eyes is missing as a result of the sun's blow.

Being married, the sun and moon travel together in the same direction, with the moon leading. When the moon gets tired, the sun catches up with her and carries her for two days. During that time people do not see the moon at all. On the third day the moon is left at the sun's setting place. On the fourth day the donkeys begin to see the sliver of the new moon and bray at her. Only on the fifth day do the people and their cattle behold the moon once again.

When a new moon appears, the Masai throw a twig or stone at it with their left hand and say, "Give me a long life," or "Give me strength." A pregnant woman might say, "Moon, give me my child safely." She puts some milk into a small gourd, which she covers with green grass, and then pours the milk in the direction of the new moon as an offering.

A halo around the moon means that a place in the skies has been attacked and that a large number of cattle have been captured. The halo is the cattle kraal. The Milky Way is the road over which the warriors are taking their captured cattle.

People believe the moon dies during an eclipse. Warriors, old men, women, and children gather outside their huts. One man chants in a loud voice, mourning the loss of the moon. Everybody joins in. "Moon, come to life again," they pray. "Moon, come to life again." They continue chanting until the moon reappears. Then everyone returns to his hut and goes to sleep.

In an eclipse of the sun the people do the same thing, and chant, "Sun, come to life again. Sun, come to life again."

The Masai's knowledge of the weather has been acquired through personal observations as well as through hearsay. If the sunrise is red, it will rain.

When the sun sets and the sky is red, they say that some warriors are out raiding and have been successful. When a rainbow appears in the sky, they know it will stop raining. Children call a rainbow "Father's dress," because it has many colors, like the handsome multicolored capes worn by the elders.

The stars, too, are related to the all-important rains. The six visible stars in the Pleiades are six head of cattle, following one another. The Pleiades are over Masailand from September until mid-May, the rainy season. This is why they are considered bringers of rain. When the Pleiades are no longer visible, people know that the rains are over.

In the constellation of Orion, the three stars in Orion's sword are considered to be three old men. The three stars in the belt of Orion are three widows. The Masai believe that the widows are pursuing the three old men.

When Venus appears, they know that dawn is near. So Venus is called the star of the dawn.

Women pray to Venus that their men will return
safely from a raid. They have two names for this
planet: Kileghen, when seen in the morning, and
Leghen, when seen in the evening.

From childhood a Masai learns the prayers and

chants, the ceremonies and dances, by watching the medicine men direct these observances and by watching the behavior of the other adults. Medicine men are held in great regard. Their insignia, although few and simple, are old and revered. They consist of an iron club, a medicine horn, a gourd, and a kidskin bag, in which sacred stones are kept. So far no European has been privileged to see them. These insignia are the medicine man's charms, which connect him with the supernatural world. They give him curing power and the ability to foretell the future.

The office of medicine man is hereditary. A father who is a medicine man passes his knowledge and insignia on to his oldest son. If he has no sons, he will pass them to his nearest male relative.

But this has not always been the case. At the turn of the century a powerful medicine man lay dying. His younger son, Lenana, who wanted very much to become a medicine man, came secretly to his bedside, pretending he was the oldest son, and got his father's insignia and his blessing. "Thou shalt be great amongst thy brothers and all the people," the old medicine man prophesied for his son.

Lenana told the elders of the clan that his three brothers, Sendeyo, Neliang, and Tolito, had talked with their father prior to his death and that the father had said Lenana would make the best medicine man. But, he said, the father did not wish to appoint him, because it was against custom. The elders then chose Lenana, because they agreed that he had more knowledge and power and would make the best medicine man.

The oldest son, Sendeyo, and the warriors of his age set rose up in arms against Lenana. Sendeyo said, "I will not be subject to my brother. I will fight him until I kill him."

The brothers and their followers fought. After the turn of the century such wars between brother clans were forbidden, but it was not unusual in the early days for one group of Masai to fight among themselves, raid and steal cattle, and shed each other's blood. Finally, after years of fighting, Sendeyo gave up and recognized his brother as leader and as medicine man. Victorious, Lenana now held the iron club of office.

The Masai do not like to speak of the dead, and they never mention the names of deceased persons. They do not mourn the dead. Since ancient times they have left their dead in the open, to be eaten by hyenas and vultures. They believe that if they bury the dead, the earth will be poisoned and no grass will grow on it. They believe that when a person dies, everything has ended for him. Death is final.

However, long ago a wise man, named Le-eyo, despaired about death and wanted to bring people to life again. He wanted especially to bring back his dead children. The god told Le-eyo that the next time a child died and its body was laid outside the enclosure, he was to say, "Man, die and come back again. Moon, die and stay away."

Soon after Le-eyo received his instructions from the god, a child died in the camp. As it was carried out to be laid in the field outside the enclosure, Le-eyo had a change of mind. He feared that if the moon failed to come, there would be terrible darkness. The child was not his. So he said instead, "Man, die and stay away. Moon, die and return." When Le-eyo returned to his own hut, he found that one of his own children had died. He carried it out into the field and said, "Man, die and return. Moon, die and stay away." But the child did not revive. Le-eyo heard the god say, "You have spoiled it for all mankind by not following my words in the first place. Now nobody will return from the dead. But the moon will come back each night."

While the Masai do not believe in ghosts, they do fear evil spirits. They would rather meet a lion than an evil spirit. A lion is easily frightened or

can be killed with a flying spear hurled by a skill-
ful warrior, but the devil is far more dangerous.

When a camp is moving, everyone is warned to
be careful and to listen well, especially in dense
growth or forest. Should they hear a voice calling,
they must remain silent. It may be a devil chop-
ping a tree. They might hear him calling for help
to a warrior. "Come, brother, help me lift this load
of firewood." A kind man is sometimes lured by
this cry for help. But as soon as he gets near the
devil, he is struck on the head with a club, and the
devil cries out, "I belong to the Aiser clan. Try to
escape me if you can." Always hungry, the devil
immediately devours the person.

Medicine men, whose ears are very keen, hear a
devil before anyone else does and warn the people
when one is around. The women and children
crowd together. The warriors form a circle around
them, and the camp moves on in deep silence.

The Masai believe they live in a world that is
surrounded by both evil and good spirits. No one

has control over these spirits. The evil ones, of course, do evil to the Masai. But whereas in our stories the good fairies always bring about justice, in the Masai stories even the good spirits sometimes bring evil. Perhaps that is why some Masai stories seem to us unnecessarily cruel.

The Masai relate very simply the legend of how they came into existence. When the wise man Le-eyo grew old and lay dying, he called his two surviving sons to him and asked the older one what he would like to have. The older son said he wanted something of everything on earth: some cattle, a few goats and sheep, and some food of the earth. Le-eyo then called his second son and asked him what he wanted. The youngster said, "Father, all I want is the fan which you carry in your hand as a remembrance of you." Le-eyo was touched by his son's modesty and blessed him. "Son," he said, "God shall give you wealth, and you will be the greatest of your people."

And so it came to pass. The older son got a little

of everything on earth. His descendants became the numerous Bantu herders and farmers. The younger son's descendants are the Masai.

The stories the Masai tell their children carry on their traditions and beliefs. There are hundreds of such tales about everything that concerns Masai life: about raids, wars, jealousy among wives, fights among warriors, good and bad treatment of children. There are many, many animal stories. From childhood to maturity, people listen to these tales over and over again. No matter how familiar it is, a storyteller always relates his story from beginning to end, never willingly omitting a single detail.

Masai legends differ from ours, because they are a different people, with different ways of thinking and acting and with different values. Stories about birds and the sky, about rain and tall trees, are told with reverence, because these things are respected by the people. They also tell stories about tricksters. In our stories, tricksters always get their comeuppance. In Masai stories, this is not always so. However, the way the Masai obtained their cattle by trickery seems justified to them, since a Dorobo was responsible for much of the mischief.

In the Masai beliefs, the sky and the earth were one in ancient times. The god Enkai lived among men and talked with them. But one day a Dorobo hunter shot an arrow at Enkai. Angered, the god separated the sky from the earth and went to live permanently in the sky.

When Enkai came down to see the world, he found in the land a Dorobo man, an elephant, a serpent, and a milch cow, all living together. One day the Dorobo asked the serpent, "Friend, why do I itch when you breathe on me?" The serpent said he was sorry, but he did not blow his breath on the Dorobo on purpose. The Dorobo, however, was not satisfied with the serpent's apology. When night came and the serpent fell asleep, the Dorobo grabbed his club and smashed the serpent's head.

The following day the elephant missed her

friend, the serpent. "Where is the thin one?" she asked the Dorobo. The Dorobo explained that he had to kill the serpent, because he could not stand his breath.

It rained heavily that day, and the Dorobo took his cow out to graze and to wallow in all the fresh puddles. They stayed away for three days until the rain puddles began to dry up. When they returned they found that the elephant had given birth and had gone to graze, drink, and wallow in the last puddle that was left. The next day, when the Dorobo went out to graze his cow, the puddle was too muddy for drinking. So the Dorobo killed the mother elephant. The baby elephant escaped and ran to the lands of the Masai. He met a warrior and told him that he could not live with the bad Dorobo who had killed his mother.

The Masai made the young elephant repeat his tale twice, to be sure he understood it and would not be guilty of a hasty act. Then he picked up his shield and spear and said, "Let's go. I should like to meet this Dorobo."

They found the Dorobo's kraal, but he was not at home. His hut had been overturned, so that the door faced the sky. Then the Masai and the baby elephant heard the god Enkai call to the Dorobo, because he thought the Dorobo was at home. "I wish you to come tomorrow morning, for I have something to tell you," Enkai said.

The Dorobo, not being there, missed the order. Instead, the Masai warrior appeared before the god the next day. Thinking he was the Dorobo, the god said, "Build a big kraal and slaughter a calf." The Masai found a calf, killed it, and fastened the hide outside the door, as he had been told to do. He did not eat the meat, but threw it into the fire as a sacrifice. Then he and the baby elephant hid inside the hut.

Huddled there, they heard the thunder of a thousand hoofs. A long strip of the hide had been cut to connect the heavens and earth. At once cattle began to descend along the strip, one by one. Soon the large kraal was entirely filled with cattle, pressing against one another and against the thorny wall of the kraal and the dry wall of the hut. Inside the hut, the Masai warrior was afraid that he and the elephant would be crushed. Never before had he seen so many head of cattle. Frightened, he cried out.

At his outcry, the strip of hide was cut. The cattle stopped descending. The warrior heard Enkai say, "This will be enough cattle for you. You are to care for them, and you will get no more, since you have shown surprise and cried out."

From that day on, the Masai have had cattle and have been caring for them. Neither the Dorobo nor any of the other people of Africa received any cattle. This is why, when the Masai see herds of cattle among their Dorobo and Bantu neighbors, they believe that the cattle came from the herd given them by Enkai.

THE MASAI TODAY

The Masai fear comets. When they see one they say, "Great trouble will come. Cattle will die. There will be a famine." Just before the Europeans arrived a comet appeared. Also a green ox was supposedly seen by some children at a water hole when they came to water their cattle. They killed the green ox. It had no blood, just fat. The medicine men, when they heard of this, predicted that people of green color would soon invade their land. Soon after this, less than a century later, the Europeans came to Masailand.

For a time Africa was divided up among many European powers—the Germans, the Italians, the British, the Belgians, the French, the Spanish, and the Portuguese. In their travels and contacts with other Africans the Masai warriors brought back tales of changes caused by these European settlers. They learned that European governments drafted people for work on roads and as carriers for safaris. Africans also had to pay taxes to the new governments. They had to sell their produce to visitors. The Masai did not want to work for anyone except their own families. They did not want to sell their cattle, no matter how high the price Europeans wished to pay. Cattle were the only wealth the Masai valued.

In Africa all white people, whether born in Europe, Africa, or America, are called Europeans. The Masai call them 'L-Ojuju, which means hairy. They used to say, "We have never seen people who look like you." During the past fifty years the Masai have seen many Europeans, at Nairobi in Kenya, at Dar es Salaam, capital of Tanganyika, and on their own reserves. But they still call a European 'L-Ojuju before they learn his given name.

Already the Europeans have made deep changes in some Masai ways. The British government forbade warfare and raiding. The British are proud that they have stopped intertribal warfare and cattle raids and have brought peace to the Masai tribesmen. This, however, took important goals away from the Masai.

It is true that the British have tried to be fair and to respect as many other Masai traditions as possible. They promised that the Masai could keep the reserves assigned to them and that no one would trespass on them. They also assured the Masai that they could keep their cattle, and they tried to help them save their herds from disease.

For centuries the Masai used simple remedies and charms to cure animal sicknesses caused by hoof-and-mouth disease, rinderpest, and the tsetse fly. When the herds moved into regions to the south that were infested with the tsetse fly, they were almost wiped out. And the Masai still recall the rinderpest epidemic that struck their cattle in 1890, almost destroying them completely. Whatever has been done toward conquering these diseases has come from the Europeans. And this is one medicine—cures for their cattle—that the Masai accept readily.

Each year the Europeans are making more and more progress in fighting the fatal cattle disease caused by the tsetse fly, but it is not completely conquered yet. The tsetse thrives on game animals in the bush country. A fly matures a large grub inside it. Within a few minutes after the fly lays the grub, the grub turns into a tough pupa, which cannot be destroyed easily by sprays. The tsetse kills Masai cattle and causes sleeping sickness in man, although it is not fatal to wildlife, which often become carriers. To keep the tsetse fly from re-entering areas that have been cleared, it is best to

cultivate the ground. Yet the Masai refuse to let a plow touch their lands. "Grass is sacred and not meant for the plow," they say.

Before research proved that not all game animals acted as hosts to the tsetse fly, everyone assumed that in order to kill this pest all wildlife must be destroyed. Soon the herds of buffalo, the giraffe, the wildebeest, the waterbuck, and the impala began to be exterminated in northern Tanganyika. Elsewhere European hunters on safaris helped considerably to empty and silence the African plains. In a matter of only fifty years over a hundred species of wildlife were wiped out, and the remaining number reduced.

Today the cry from everywhere is to preserve as much as possible of this magnificent wilderness for future generations. The problem remains of how to do it and yet permit the full use of the land by the Masai and other Africans. Setting up animal reserves has helped, but even in these reserves there is much poaching by both Africans and Europeans.

However, despite unfavorable conditions, wild species multiply much faster than domestic cattle. Studies have shown that wild game can survive in areas where there is not enough food for domesticated animals, because they eat a greater variety of plants, and some, such as certain types of antelope, can live without water for an amazingly long time.

When the grass in a pasture becomes overgrazed, the people drive their herds to the hills. They stealthily burn sections of forest to open it up to grazing. The fires they start thus destroy ever larger areas. Fires in these hot, dry lands burn for a long time. After the surface growth has burned, the fire continues to smolder underground, destroying tree roots and shrubs that hold the topsoil. Without adequate grass cover, hilltops are soon eroded by winds and rain. So the lands of the Masai are turning to desert. It is now forbidden to burn the forests in order to get more grassland for their cattle. The Masai must cut the size of their herds, but to them this is as yet unthinkable.

Another threat to the Masai grasslands comes from other Africans who need more land for farming. These farmers worm their way in. A Kikuyu gets permission to plant a small field on the rim of a Masai pasture and, in return, promises to share with the owner the millet and yams he plans to grow on it. Gradually more and more Kikuyu and Luo farmers come across the Masai borders. They bring their families and settle permanently.

Now that Tanganyika is independent, it is very likely that the government will win public approval for gaining control of Masailand. The argument of the land hungry is, "Isn't it more important to plant crops, which will feed more people, than to raise a few sheep and goats?"

Today the 235,000,000 people in Africa still speak almost 1000 languages. They are farmers, cattlemen, fruit growers, miners, and fishermen. The color of their skins varies from very dark to the light brown of the Masai and the white of the North Africans.

On the whole, Africa, which stretches 5000 miles from north to south and holds a fifth of the earth's surface, is a poor continent. Its mineral wealth is concentrated in only a few countries. The rest are so poor in mineral wealth that they cannot hope for the relatively rapid prosperity that comes with industrialization. Of the continent's water supply, 65% is in the Congo and nearby equatorial Africa. So the need for water holds back at least half of Africa's land mass from profitable use.

Commerce is in the hands of Asian immigrants, who number less than one million. There are over five million Europeans in Africa, plus another one and a half million people who are a mixture of European and African.

As to religion, only slightly over 40 million of Africa's 235 million people are Christians; 90 million are Moslems. The other Africans feel closer to the Moslems, perhaps because they have known the Arabs longer and perhaps, too, because the Moslems accept polygamy. Even though the Arabs once carried off thousands of people into slavery, the Masai resent the recent experiences under white colonialism more.

People all over Africa have begun to talk of independence. African people feel they deserve freedom, equality, and self-government as do the nations over the rest of the world. So they have turned to the United Nations to seek justice. When they feel that the United Nations is too slow in coming to decisions, too slow to act, some of them take matters into their own hands and revolt. Confusion, hatred, looting, destruction of property, and bloodshed have occurred in Kenya, the Congo, and Algeria.

Thus swift changes have come about in Africa. Whereas in 1950 there were only four independent states in Africa—Liberia, Ethiopia, Egypt, and the Union of South Africa—by the end of 1961 there were twenty-nine African states. Of these, Tanganyika, where most of the Masai now live, became independent on December 9, 1961. This young state was spared strife and bloodshed. Its entry into the free world of nations was accomplished peacefully, solely through votes.

There are still some twenty-three countries in Africa awaiting independence, among them Kenya. So again a group of the Masai will have their own government instead of living in a British colony.

The struggle for statehood and world recognition is just beginning to interest the Masai. Today they still follow their original ways more closely than any other African group. The people still dress as of old. Men wear colorful blankets, cotton capes, and sandals of buffalo hide. They still rub their bodies with grease made of sheep's fat and red ocher. They still wear all their iron ornaments, earrings, and strings of beads. The men still say, "Cattle are in our hearts. Their smell is sweet to us." They continue to herd their cattle for the night in kraals with thorn fences. Wives and children pick the ticks off the animals daily before sending them to pasture. Sprays are available, but few Masai use them. The men are still proud and self-reliant, and ready to hurl their formidable spears at any hostile trespasser, whether a lion or a man.

The Masai have begun to prepare themselves for the coming fight over their lands. The elders want their bright young men to go to Europe and America to learn Western languages and laws, so they will be prepared to defend their old land rights. Thirty years ago it was reported that there was only one Masai boy in a primary school in Kenya. Today several schools for Masai children have been opened in Kenya and Tanganyika. More schools are planned.

The Masai youngsters are taught geography, the history of their people and their country, science, health, agriculture, animal husbandry, and handicrafts. Girls also learn domestic science. Both boys and girls have learned to accept the different manner of living, working, and eating they find in school. They like to bathe daily and are

comfortable in the school dress of shorts and shirts for boys and skirts and blouses for girls.

To make the schools more attractive to Masai youngsters, the teachers have divided the students into age sets. Each age set chooses a boy to represent them as a kind of spokesman. They now call him a prefect, and the children feel free to come to him with their complaints.

The biggest problem is language. It is hard to find enough teachers to carry the youngsters through the first few months of their schooling in their own language. After that Swahili is introduced, for this is the language the Masai speak with outsiders, both African and European. European languages are introduced in the third grade. Once the children master a European language, it is easier to get books for them, even though these books present additional difficulties. They are based on European life and values, which are totally unfamiliar to African children and which confuse them.

The governments are trying to train native

teachers as fast as they can, and there are Masai students in America and in Europe. Already there are some Masai lawyers, teachers, medical doctors, and veterinarians. But there are still too few of them to meet the needs of almost 115,000 people.

When the railway that runs to Nairobi and east to the coast on the Indian Ocean was building a pipeline from Mount Kilimanjaro, several Masai elders approached the engineers and asked them to set up watering points for the cattle along the route. The engineers agreed, provided the Masai introduced pasture management. To this the local Masai agreed, and they fenced in some of their grazing lands. The quality of their bulls has improved. They now get more milk from their cows than ever before. Teams of schoolboys and herders have begun to plant trees in badly eroded areas to keep the land from slipping away.

In the meantime, conservationists the world over have been studying the best ways and means to conserve wilderness areas. Some say that it is not good, in the long run, to try to change the land

MASAILAND

by clearing it and planting grass, no matter how much it is needed by the people who depend on cattle for survival. In the long run, conservationists believe, it is better to preserve the balance among natural grasslands, wildlife, and cattle, than to try to change everything.

The Ngorongoro Conservation Area, for example, which covers 2500 square miles in northeastern Tanganyika, was established in 1959 by the British government. Ngorongoro has been turned over entirely to the Masai. Only about fifty park personnel were left there to enforce the laws concerning visitors to the area. The park personnel want the Masai to make full use of the region. Another recently acquired area, the Amboseli Reserve in southern Kenya, was also turned over to the Masai as their tribal park.

For the present it has been suggested that some of the money received by the parks administration for hunting licenses and tourist fees be paid to the Masai. It has been necessary in the reserves to cut down the number of game animals, when some of them have grown too abundant for their pastures and have threatened to overgraze them. Some of the meat and the income from the sale of this meat, too, might be turned over to the Masai. Money also comes in for ivory found on the reserves and for the sale of hides and skins. If this, too, were turned over to the Masai, it would help tide the people over the experimental period, until better grazing methods are introduced.

East Africa is no less exciting today than it was a hundred years ago, when the first European visitors arrived. People are striving toward complete independence. Everyone is working toward a better future. Hope runs high on the winds of change. A visitor soon forgets the discomfort of the red dust, the heat, and the insects of the East African lowlands. What is remembered is the vastness of its horizons, its earthy smells, the simplicity of life, the peace, beauty, and restfulness of the open spaces, the strange and varied wildlife and, of course, its people.

Meanwhile, the Masai are progressing at their

own rate of speed. Whether they will end up as cattlemen or farmers—or both—these free and noble people still cherish their old ways and the parts of their culture that mean the most to them. These brave warriors and raiders may yet prove to be the most successful of all Africans at achieving a life of peace and freedom.

INDEX

*Indicates illustrations